Sheep

Sheep

by Christina Wilsdon

Reader's
Digest

Published by The Reader's Digest Association, Inc.

London • New York • Sydney • Montreal

CONTENTS

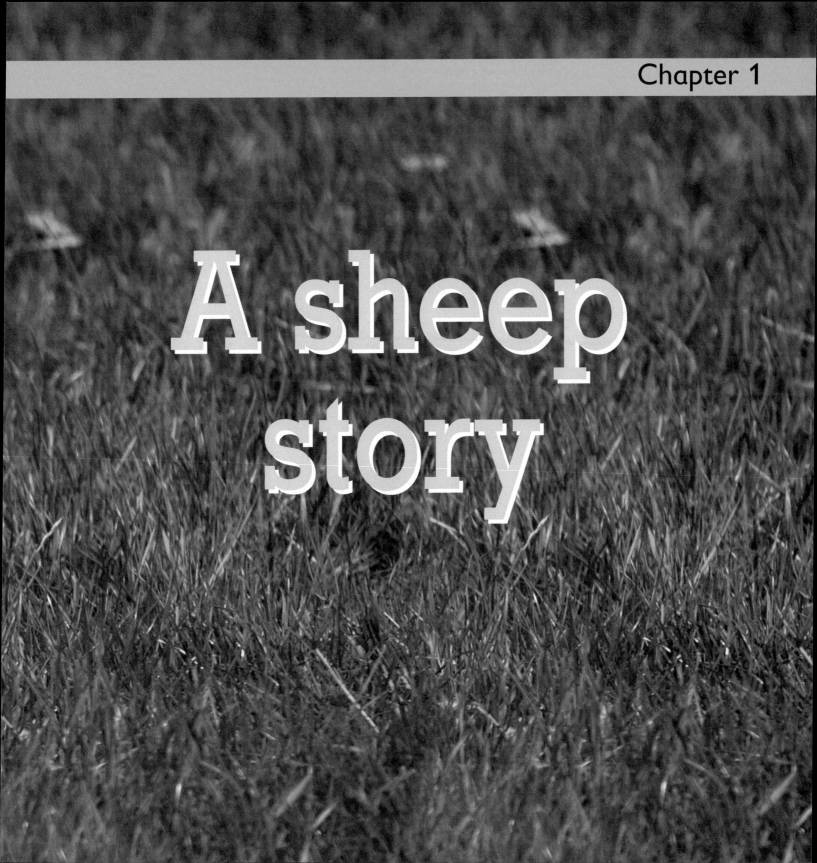

Chapter 1

A sheep story

A flock of fluffy sheep moved slowly across the field of the small farm. Every sheep was busy eating grass. Every sheep, that is, except Mother Sheep.

Mother Sheep felt too restless to eat. She knew that her baby would soon be born. By the end of the day, she would have a new lamb skipping at her side.

Mother Sheep wandered back to the barn. She went inside and found a pen full of straw. With her front legs, she dug until she had made a little nest. Then she lay down in it.

A few hours later, Baby Lamb arrived. He lay in the straw while Mother Sheep licked him from head to toe.

'Baa, baa,' she murmured as she scrubbed him clean. She nudged him with her nose. The little lamb stood up and took his first wobbly steps. Mother Sheep nuzzled him as he drank his first meal of milk.

Spotted sheep

Jacob sheep have a coat of white wool with black spots. The black wool grows a bit longer than the white wool!

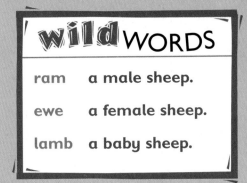

wild WORDS

ram	a male sheep.
ewe	a female sheep.
lamb	a baby sheep.

For a few days, Mother Sheep and Baby Lamb stayed together in the pen. The farmer kept them separated from the other sheep to make sure Mother Sheep could bond with her baby and give him her best milk.

'Baaaa', said Baby Lamb in a high-pitched voice. Mother Sheep replied with a deep, long 'baaaa'. Baby Lamb knew the sound of Mother Sheep's call, just as Mother Sheep knew his. Knowing the sound of each other's voice will help them to find one another in the flock.

Mother Sheep was a good mother. She had raised a few sets of twins over the years. This was the first time she had given birth to just one baby. But caring for even one lamb was plenty of work.

wild WORDS

bleat   the high *baa* sound that a lamb makes.

The tail's end

Why do many sheep have short tails? Farmers often remove part of a lamb's tail soon after birth. This is called docking. Tails are docked to help keep sheep clean and stop flies from bothering them.

Sometimes when lambs play together, they practise skills they will need later in life, such as head butting.

When Mother Sheep and Baby Lamb left the pen after a few days, they joined a group of other ewes and lambs. At first Baby Lamb stayed close to his mother but soon he discovered that other lambs were fun to play with. He left Mother Sheep's side and ran and skipped with them. When he was tired or hungry, he scampered back to his mother.

Baby Lamb's main food was his mother's milk. He also ate feed that the farmer put out for the lambs. The farmer put the feed into a pen that was just the right size for the lambs to go into, but too small for the ewes to get into.

Baby Lamb grew quickly. He weighed about 3kg when he was born. By the time he was ten weeks old, he weighed more than 20kg. He was ready to start eating plants like his mother.

Little lamb games

A ewe is patient with her lambs – even when they try to climb onto her back.

Chapter 2

A sheep's body

Full of wool

Sheep have woolly coats, which help to keep them warm. It is a kind of curly hair, which other animals have, too, but it grows especially long and thick in most sheep.

Many sheep grow white or cream-coloured wool, but it can be black, grey, brown, tan or spotted. Sheep's faces and legs may be a different colour from their body, too. A Suffolk sheep has a black face and legs. A California Red sheep's legs and face are rusty. A Welsh Mountain sheep's dark face has a white stripe from its eyes to its nose.

No wool

 Some kinds of sheep do not grow thick woolly coats. They are called hair sheep. Farmers raise hair sheep in places where the weather is very hot, such as in parts of Africa. These sheep provide milk and meat.

Hair sheep do not need wool to stay warm. If winter gets too cold, the sheep will grow thick coats of hair to keep warm. In spring, they will shed the extra hair.

There are more than 200 different kinds, or breeds, of sheep. Most have white or cream-coloured wool. Others have wool that is a different colour or two-toned. Some have no wool at all!

Sheep look very different without their woolly coats.

Sheep shapes

A sheep has a sturdy body and strong, thin legs. Each hoof is made up of two hard toes. This kind of hoof is called a split hoof. Goats have split hoofs, too. A split hoof helps sheep and goats to walk, leap and climb in rocky places.

Sheep have big ears that can swivel in all directions, which help them to pick up sounds. They can flare their nostrils to sniff the air for danger. Beneath the nostrils is a line that leads to the sheep's upper lip. The split upper lip helps sheep to pluck blades of grass to eat.

Sheep or goat?

Some kinds of sheep look a lot like goats. But you can tell them apart by looking for a few clues. A male goat may have a beard. A ram does not. A goat has straight horns. A ram usually has curled horns. Many female goats have horns, but many ewes do not. A goat's tail is often flipped up, but a sheep's tail usually hangs down.

If you can't tell which is which by using your eyes, try your other senses. Listen to the animal's sound. A sheep makes a sound like 'baa', while a goat's sound is like 'maa'. Goats also smell more strongly than sheep.

Head of horns

Many kinds of sheep grow horns. In some breeds, only the ram grows horns. In other breeds, both the ram and ewe grow horns, but the ram's horns are bigger. Some breeds of sheep do not grow horns at all. Sheep that do not grow horns are called 'polled'.

A few kinds of sheep grow more than one pair of horns. Jacob sheep rams and ewes can grow four horns and some of them even grow six horns!

The outer layer of a sheep's horn is made of the same material that forms your hair and fingernails. The inside layer of the horn is made of bone.

People have long used sheep horns to make things, such as buttons and spoons. Horns are even used as instruments to make sounds. Blowing into a hollow horn makes a sound like a trumpet.

Sheep use their horns to protect themselves. Rams also use their horns to fight other rams. A ram's thick skull protects his head when he crashes his horns against another ram's head. The ram locks horns with the other ram and pushes and twists to knock him down.

A ram's horns are hollow inside and make loud sounds when air is blown into them. In ancient times, people used ram horns to communicate with others who lived far away.

21

Chapter 3

What sheep do

Laze and graze

Sheep spend much of the day eating. They graze on grass, weeds and other plants in fields.

A sheep has no upper front teeth. It has a tough pad on its gums instead. It eats grass by pressing it between its lower front teeth and the pad. Then it tears the grass with a quick snap of its head. The sheep swallows the grass after barely chewing it. The food goes into two parts of its four-part stomach.

Later, the sheep coughs up a ball of grass called a cud. The sheep chews the cud with a side-to-side motion of its jaw. The cud is crushed and torn by the sheep's back teeth. Then it is swallowed. It goes into the other parts of the sheep's stomach to be digested. Meanwhile, the sheep coughs up another cud to chew.

Sheep nip off plants very close to the ground. Farmers must be careful not to let sheep spoil a pasture by feeding in it for too long, so they may be moved around to avoid overgrazing. However, sheep can also benefit the poor soil of hills and mountainsides, as their dung has a fertilising effect, so you may notice richer grass on hilly ground where sheep graze.

Sheep eat so much grass the fields don't need to be mown.

Every sheep in a flock knows its place.
Some sheep act as leaders. The other
sheep follow them to new grazing spots.

Ewe-nity

Sheep are born with a strong need to be in a group, which is called a flock. A sheep gets nervous when it is all alone. It bleats and paws the ground if it cannot at least see another sheep. This need to be in a group is called flocking behaviour.

Flocking helps sheep to survive. In a flock, sheep have many sets of eyes and ears on guard against danger. If there's any sign of danger, the sheep bunch together and run. The safest place to be is in the middle of the flock. There, a sheep is protected by the bodies of the other sheep. But even being on the edge of the flock is safer than being alone.

Flocking behaviour helps people take care of sheep. A flock learns to follow the person, called a shepherd, who takes care of them.

Sheep at rest

The way sheep eat helps to keep them safe if they live in places where wolves or other predators might attack them. They swallow food whole and chew the cuds later, which allows a sheep to quickly fill its stomach with grass when the animal is out in the open, and then chew the food carefully when it is in a safer place.

A sheep may spend hours chewing while it is lying down. A sheep can sleep standing up, just as a horse can. But it sleeps more deeply when it lies down.

Baby lambs are full of energy and run, and play with other lambs. But, like young children, they lie down to take a nap.

Rounding up the flock

A herding dog, called a sheepdog, often helps the shepherd or farmer to look after the flock. In Britain, the most common type of sheepdog is the Border Collie. These dogs are renowned for being clever, hardworking and agile, and for their innate herding skills – skills which have been developed by many generations of breeding. A well-trained dog is invaluable for gathering up sheep in hilly areas which are inaccessible to vehicles.

Every summer, sheepdog trials are held throughout Britain. This is where farmers and shepherds bring their best dogs to demonstrate their extraordinary abilities to follow their masters' instructions – often a series of commands, whistles and gestures – and round up dozens of sheep and guide them into narrow pens.

Sheepdogs

Sheepdogs are born with the ability to herd other animals, and they can be trained for specific situations. The dog runs around the flock and takes control. Even just a hard stare from a sheepdog can get a flock moving.

Chapter 4

Wild sheep

Big-horned bighorns

Bighorn sheep live wild in western North America. Bighorn rams grow long, thick horns that curl. Ewes grow shorter horns.

Bighorn sheep graze in mountain meadows. Their hoofs have soft pads between the hard edges, which give bighorns a firm grip when climbing on rocks. Bighorn sheep never stray far from the safety of cliffs.

Ewes and lambs form small herds for most of the year. The rams live separately in bands made up just of rams. In autumn, rams battle with each other over mates. In winter, the sheep form bigger herds that may have up to 100 animals. An experienced ewe is the herd's leader.

Wolves, cougars, bears, bobcats and coyotes hunt bighorns. Golden eagles sometimes snatch lambs. People also hunt bighorns.

Small horns

Bighorn ewes grow shorter horns than rams do. A bighorn ewe usually has her first lamb when she is two years old. Twins are rare among bighorns.

Bighorn rams grow long, thick horns that curl.

DID YOU KNOW?

An old bighorn ram's set of horns can weigh up to 14kg – about as much as six newborn lambs!

Urials have huge curved horns – those with the largest horns tend to be leaders of the herd.

Urial sheep

Urial sheep are wild sheep which live on grassy slopes across western central Asia from northeastern Iran to Ladakh, a north Indian province on the borders of Tibet.

Urials have a reddish brown long fur, and the males also have a distinctive black ruff at the front of the neck. Both the ram and ewe grow large horns which curl outwards, but a ram's horns are much bigger — they can be almost a metre long!

The ewes and lambs form herds of related family members. Adult rams form separate all-male groups — and males with the larger horns tend to be dominant. But, in September, the males seek out the ewes and mate with four or five females who will each have one or two lambs.

Urial sheep eat mainly grass but can also eat the leaves of trees and bushes if they need to. They are very wary creatures and often feed early in the morning or in the evening, spending the day concealed under bushes or overhanging rocks to avoid predators.

Wild but not woolly

A Barbary sheep's body is covered with hair the colour of sand and stone. The hair is long and hangs from its throat like a beard. A ram's hair may grow all the way down to its front hoofs. A mane grows along the back of the Barbary sheep's neck. Both rams and ewes grow curved horns, but the ram's horns can be twice as long as the ewe's.

Barbary sheep first lived in northern Africa. Their name comes from the Latin word *barbari*, which was the name used for the people living along the northern coast of Africa at the time of the Roman Empire. Barbary sheep are also called maned sheep.

Barbary sheep live in mountainous areas of deserts. Their sandy colour helps them to blend into their environment, making it more difficult for predators, such as leopards, to see them. Barbary sheep graze during cool mornings and evenings and at night. By day, they rest in any shade they can find. They are great jumpers. From a stand-still position, Barbary sheep can leap over an obstacle 2m high!

Today, Barbary sheep live in North Africa, Europe and the southwestern United States.

Barbary sheep live
in the wild and don't
look at all like the
sheep we are used
to seeing.

Sheep
and people

Chapter 5

Have you any wool?

Sheep are best known for their wool, which is a very strong fibre, used to make carpets, blankets and clothing. Wool clothing keeps people warm. Wool is also used to make felt, tennis balls and other items.

A sheep's wool is removed by giving the sheep a haircut, which is called shearing. Most sheep are shorn with a special kind of electric razor. An experienced shearer can shear a sheep in less than 2 minutes and cuts the wool so that it comes off in one big piece, called a fleece.

Sheep's wool contains a greasy substance called lanolin. This is used in soap, creamy lotions that make skin smooth and soft, and other products.

Different kinds of sheep grow different amounts of wool. Some very woolly breeds produce more than 13.5kg of wool per sheep.

More sheep products

Some kinds, or breeds, of sheep are raised for their milk. Sheep's milk is used to make different kinds of cheese, butter, yoghurt and ice cream.

Other breeds of sheep are raised mainly for meat. Meat from sheep less than a year old is called lamb. Meat from older sheep is called mutton.

Sheep – then and now

People first began herding sheep about 7,000 years ago. But those sheep looked more like wild sheep, either urials or mouflons, than the sheep we know. Because ancient farmers favoured sheep that were extra woolly or grew fat quickly, over time, breeding produced the different kinds of sheep there are today.

Today, hundreds of breeds of sheep are raised all over the world. China raises the most sheep of any country. Australia is the second-largest sheep producer. New Zealand is also famous for its sheep. This island nation is home to about 45 million sheep. There are eleven times more sheep in New Zealand than there are people!

FAST FACTS ABOUT FARM SHEEP

SCIENTIFIC NAME	*Ovis aries*
CLASS	Mammals
ORDER	Artiodactyla
SIZE	Up to 1.2m in length
WEIGHT	Males from 68kg to 160kg Females from 45kg to 102kg
LIFE SPAN	10-20 years
HABITAT	Fields and hillsides

DID YOU KNOW?

Mouflon are wild sheep that live in parts of Europe. Although they don't look like the woolly sheep we are used to seeing today, mouflon are one of their ancestors.

GLOSSARY OF WILD WORDS

bleat	the sound a lamb makes
breeds	different varieties of the same animal species
docking	shortening a lamb's tail
domesticated	animals that have been bred over time to be farm animals and tame companions

ewe	a female sheep
feral	wild and not domesticated
fleece	a sheep's wool coat
flock	a group of sheep
hair sheep	sheep that do not grow woolly fleeces
lamb	a baby or young sheep

lanolin	greasy substance in wool	sheepdog	a dog trained to herd sheep
mutton	meat from an older sheep	shepherd	a person who tends a flock of sheep
polled	without horns		
predator	an animal that hunts and eats other animals to survive	species	a group of plants or animals that are the same in many ways
ram	a male sheep	wool	thick, fuzzy hair grown by an animal to keep it warm
shear	to cut wool off a sheep		

INDEX

CREDITS

Sheep is an ***All About Animals*** fact book
Written by Christina Wilsdon

Published in 2010 in the United Kingdom by Vivat Direct Limited (t/a Reader's Digest),
157 Edgware Road, London W2 2HR

Editor: Rachel Warren Chadd
Designer: Nicola Liddiard
Art editor: Simon Webb

Printing and binding Arvato Iberia, Portugal

ISBN: 978 0 276 44613 9
Book code: 640-022 UP0000-2
Oracle code: 504500067H.00.24